☑ None of the Above

Gerald Gardner

Tallfellow Press

Los Angeles

For Joanna, Jed, and Jonathan

Photos courtesy Corbis Images, Smithsonian Institution, Library of Congress, The White House

Copyright ©2000 by Gerald Gardner

All rights reserved. This book, or any parts thereof, may not be reproduced in any fashion whatsoever without the prior written permission of the Publisher.

Published by
Tallfellow Press, Inc.
1180 South Beverly Drive, Suite 320
Los Angeles, CA 90035

Distributed by
Andrews McMeel Distribution Services
4520 Main Street
Kansas City, Missouri 64111

Art Production by ess d&d

Printed in the USA
10 9 8 7 6 5 4 3 2 1

Introduction

President Kennedy liked this book. Well, not exactly *this* book. He liked the forerunner of this book. It was published back in 1963 and he was its chief target. Some White House wags baked some pages from the book into Kennedy's 45th birthday cake at a private party. Newsweek said he "broke up." Whether he broke up the cake or broke up about the book was never quite clear.

JFK sent me a letter saying he had enjoyed the book and invited me to visit him at the White House next time I was in Washington. He said to call his secretary, Mrs. Lincoln, for an appointment.

"I'll be in Washington on Friday," I said to her. "When can the President see me?"

"When can you make it?" said Mrs. Lincoln.

"About four?"

"Four is good."

Only in America.

She told me to enter by the Northwest Gate. At the gate I found a shack with a uniformed guard who asked to see some identification. Since I don't carry a business card, I gave him my Diners Club card. He said that was fine and snapped up the phone.

"Mr. Gardner of the Diners Club to see the President," he said.

In the Oval Office, Kennedy said that the captioned photo he liked best had an autocratic Charles de Gaulle saying to an angry looking President Eisenhower, "You're drunk!"

Kennedy had a great sense of humor. He often used his wit to laugh away the things he didn't want to talk about...

Like his father buying the election for him: "I just received this telegram from my father. He says, 'Don't buy one more vote than you need. I'll be damned if I'll pay for a landslide!'"

Like his Catholicism: "I asked Cardinal Spellman what I should say when reporters ask me about the Pope's omniscience. And he said, 'I don't know what to tell you. All I know is he keeps calling me Spillman.'"

Like appointing his brother Attorney General: "I see nothing wrong with giving Bobby a little legal experience before he goes into private practice."

A year after Kennedy's assassination, I was traveling with brother Bobby as he ran for the U.S. Senate in New York. Bobby Kennedy, surprisingly enough, was every bit as witty as his brother. His opponent in the New York Senate race was accusing him of being a Carpetbagger (funny how history repeats itself). Bobby said, "People ask me why I came to New York. Well, I was reading the newspapers the other day, and I noticed that California had passed New York in population. So I turned to my wife and I said: 'What can we do?'"

Probably the funniest man in public life was Adlai Stevenson. He told of running into a woman at the Democratic national convention. "She was eight months pregnant and she was carrying a sign that said: 'ADLAI'S THE MAN.'"

On another occasion a supporter approached him and gushed: "Every thinking person will be voting for you, Governor." And Stevenson replied: "That's not enough! We need a *majority*."

Adlai's finest hour was when he was introduced by the chairman of the Houston Baptist Convention. He was running against Ike, and the chairman said: "I should like to make it clear, Gov. Stevenson, that you are here as a *courtesy* because Dr. Norman Vincent Peale has already instructed us to vote for your opponent." Somewhat shaken, Adlai went to the mike and said, "Speaking as a Christian, I would like to say that I find the Apostle Paul appealing and the Apostle Peale appalling."

With this new book of captioned news photos, my mind goes back to that earlier president who liked the first one. This time I have focused on the *candidates* who are running for that special bit of public housing on Pennsylvania Avenue. We have rounded up the current band of suspects—George W., Al Gore, John McCain, Bill Bradley, Steve Forbes, Pat Buchanan, Donald Trump—plus other high profile pols like Hillary Rodham Clinton, Jesse Ventura et al.

As they run for their lives, I am reminded of the Secret of Getting Elected that was offered by Washington lawyer Edward Bennett Williams: Politics is the gentle art of getting votes from the poor and campaign contributions from the rich, by promising to protect each from the other.

There is one other bit of advice that was offered by Conrad Hilton on the Tonight Show during a long-ago presidential campaign. Johnny Carson said: "Conrad, I'm sure the candidates would welcome any advice you can give them. Look those candidates in the eye and tell them Life's Most Important Truth."

Hilton furrowed his brow, reflected for a moment, and said:

"Always make sure the curtain is inside the tub."

"Actually, I'd *rather* be underrated."

"It's working."

> And if China played ball, I would build the Tiananmen Trump. Three million rooms.

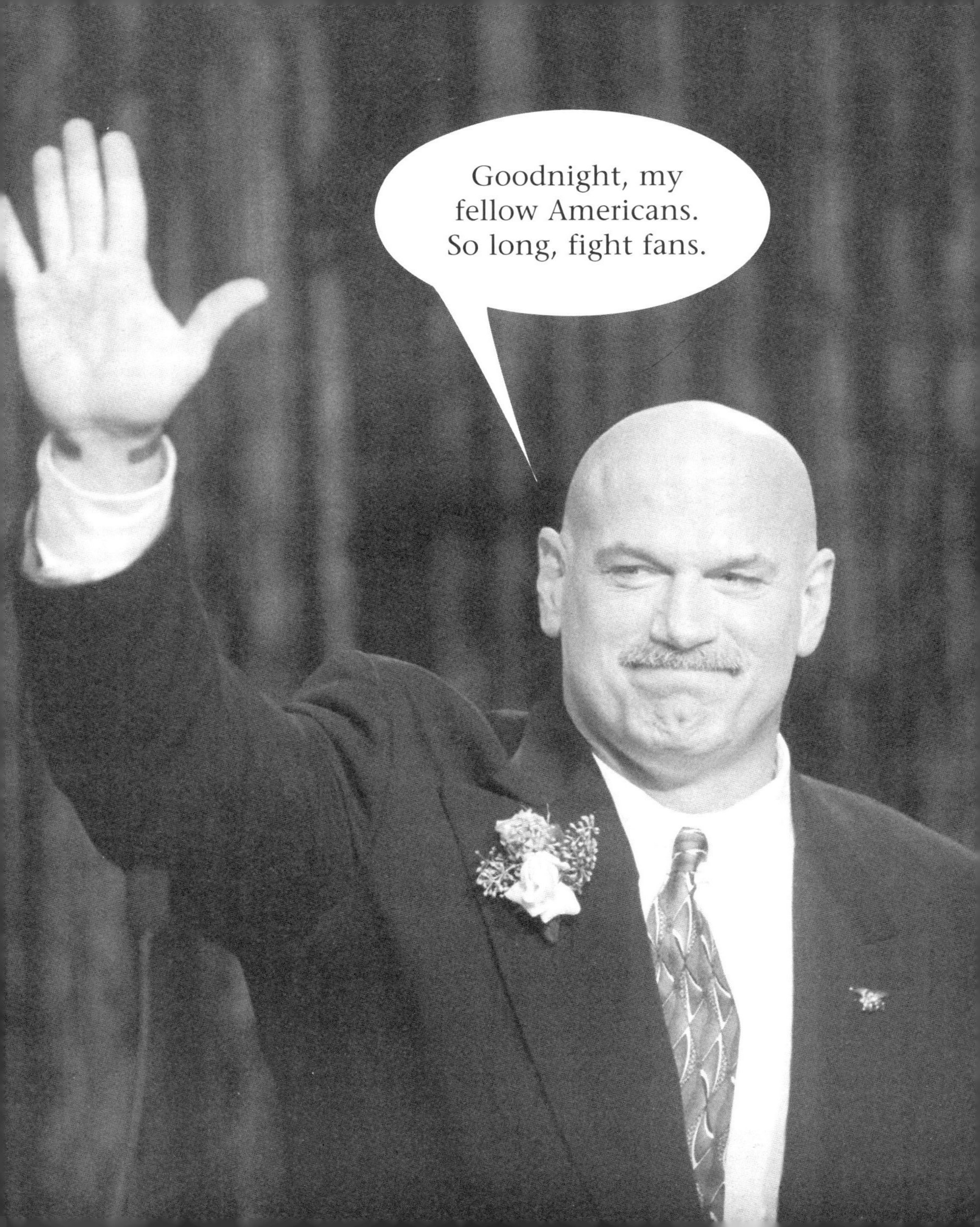
Goodnight, my fellow Americans. So long, fight fans.

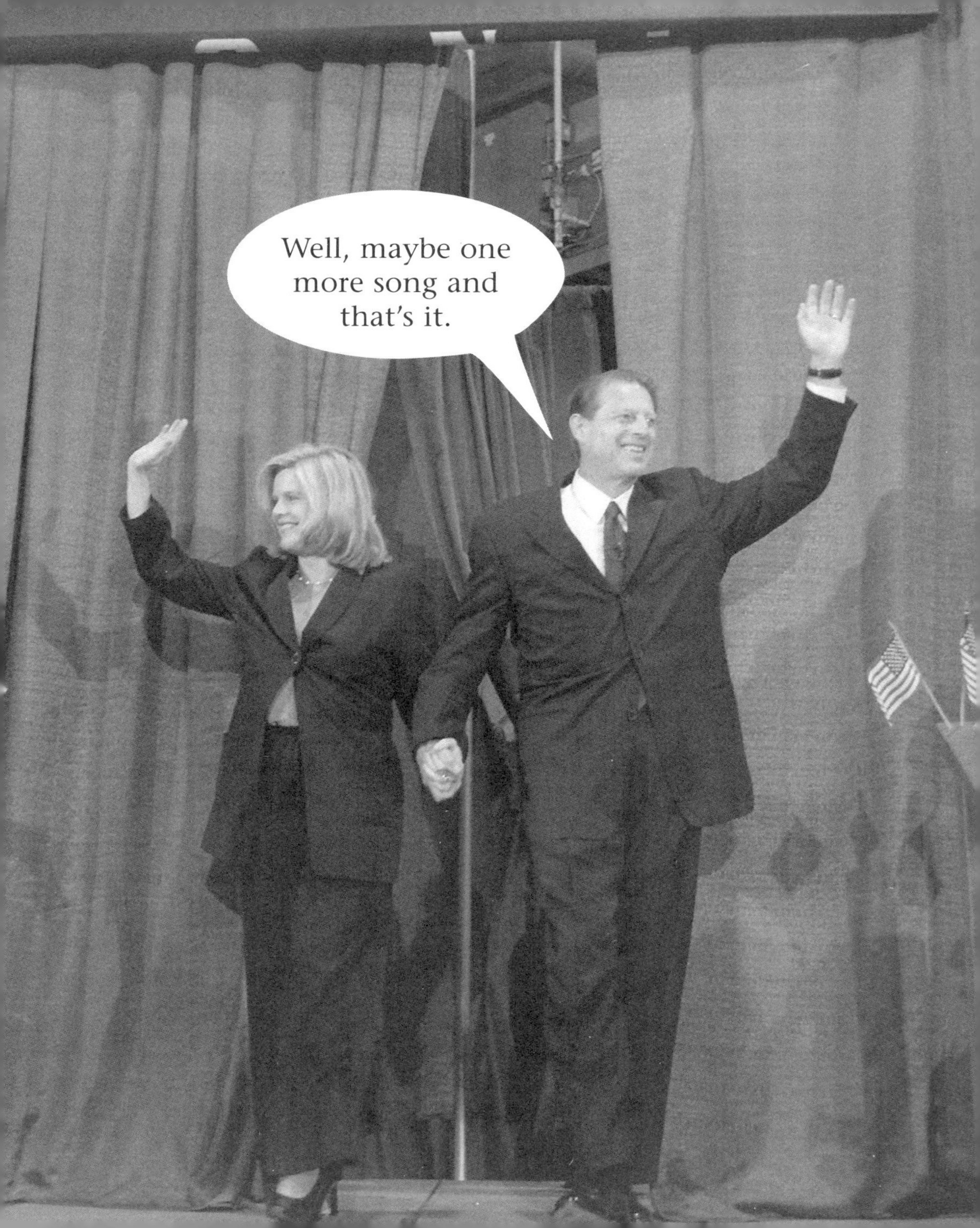
Well, maybe one more song and that's it.

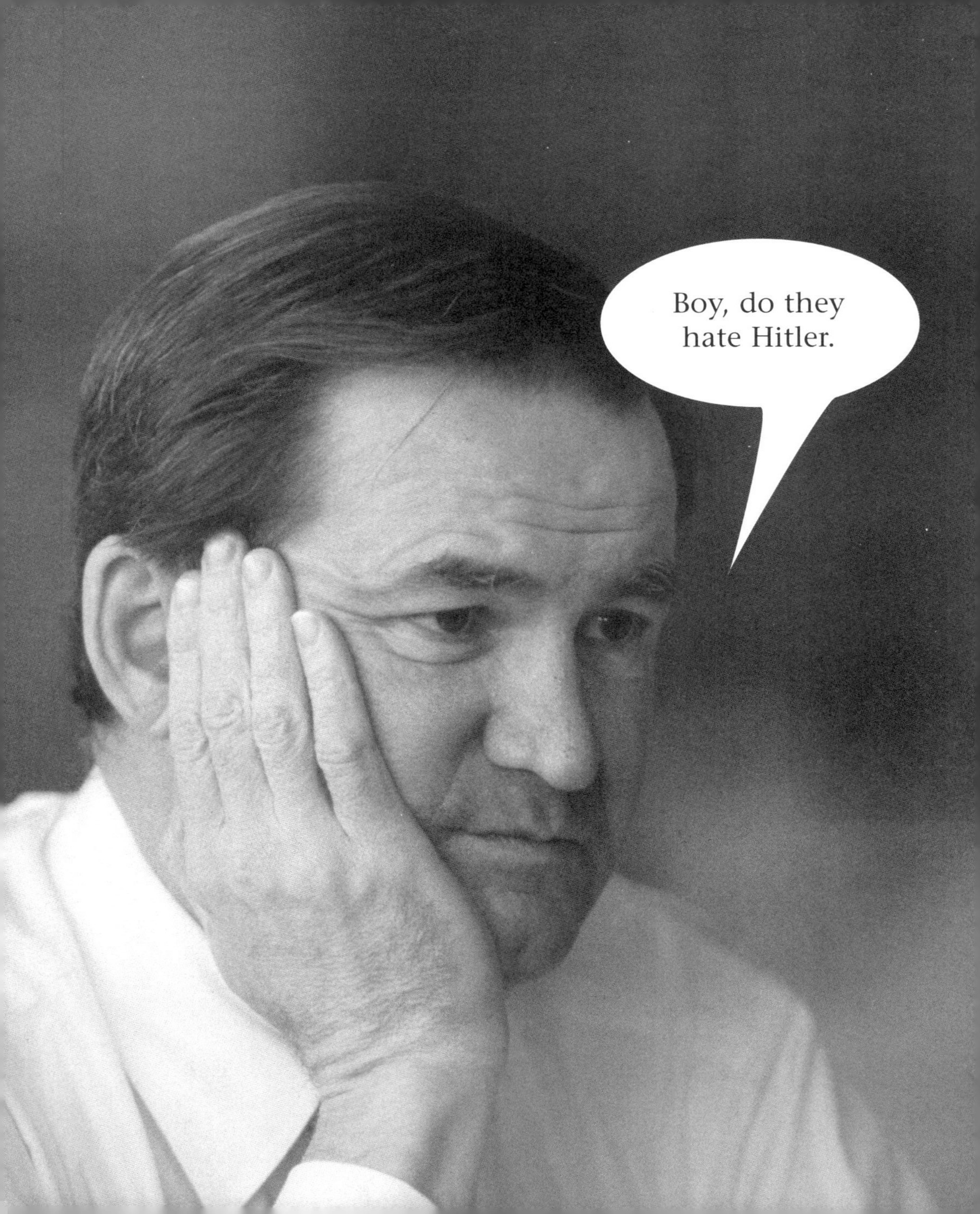
Boy, do they hate Hitler.

> George, if you can hear my voice—the president of Bulgaria is Petar Stoyanov.

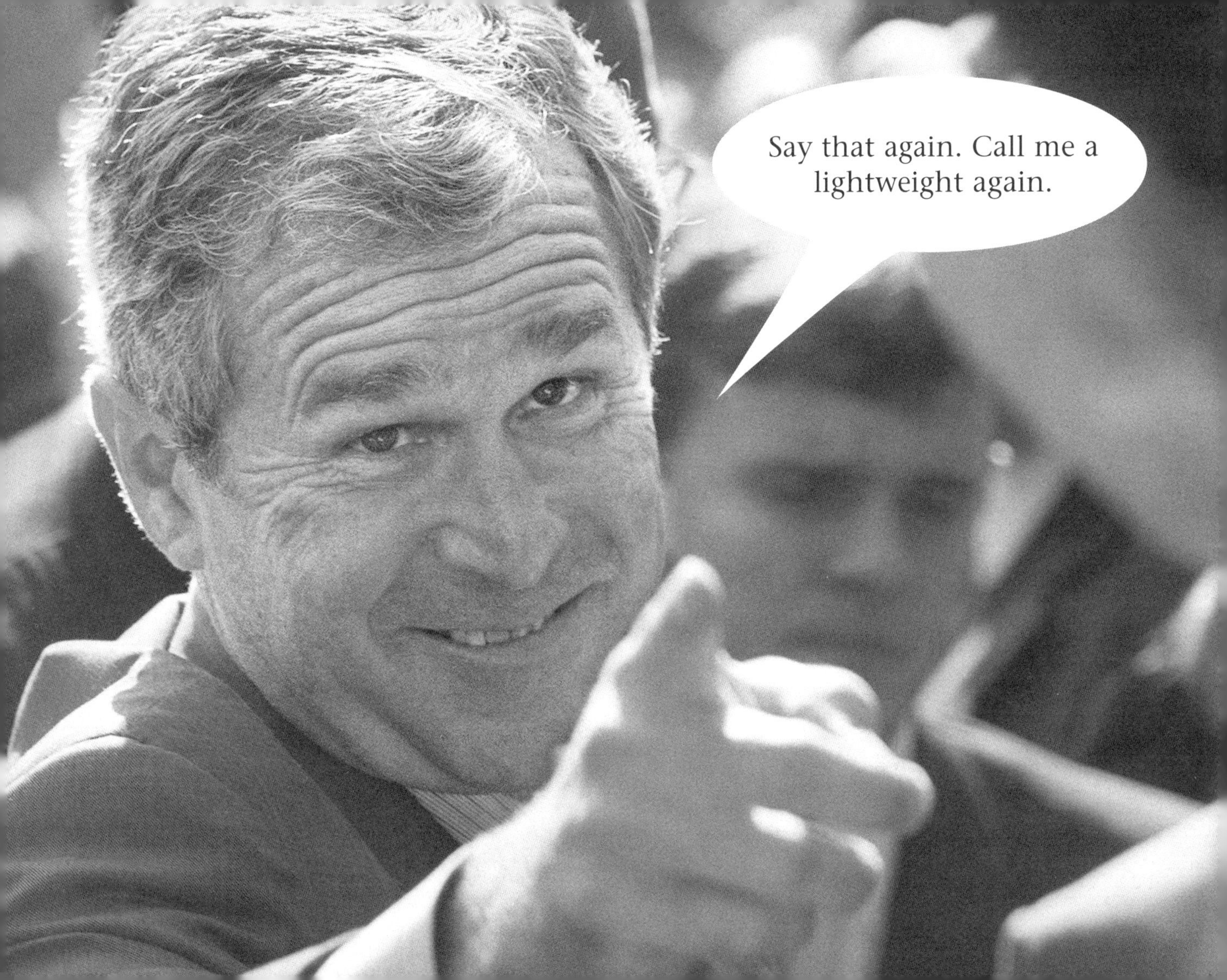
Say that again. Call me a lightweight again.

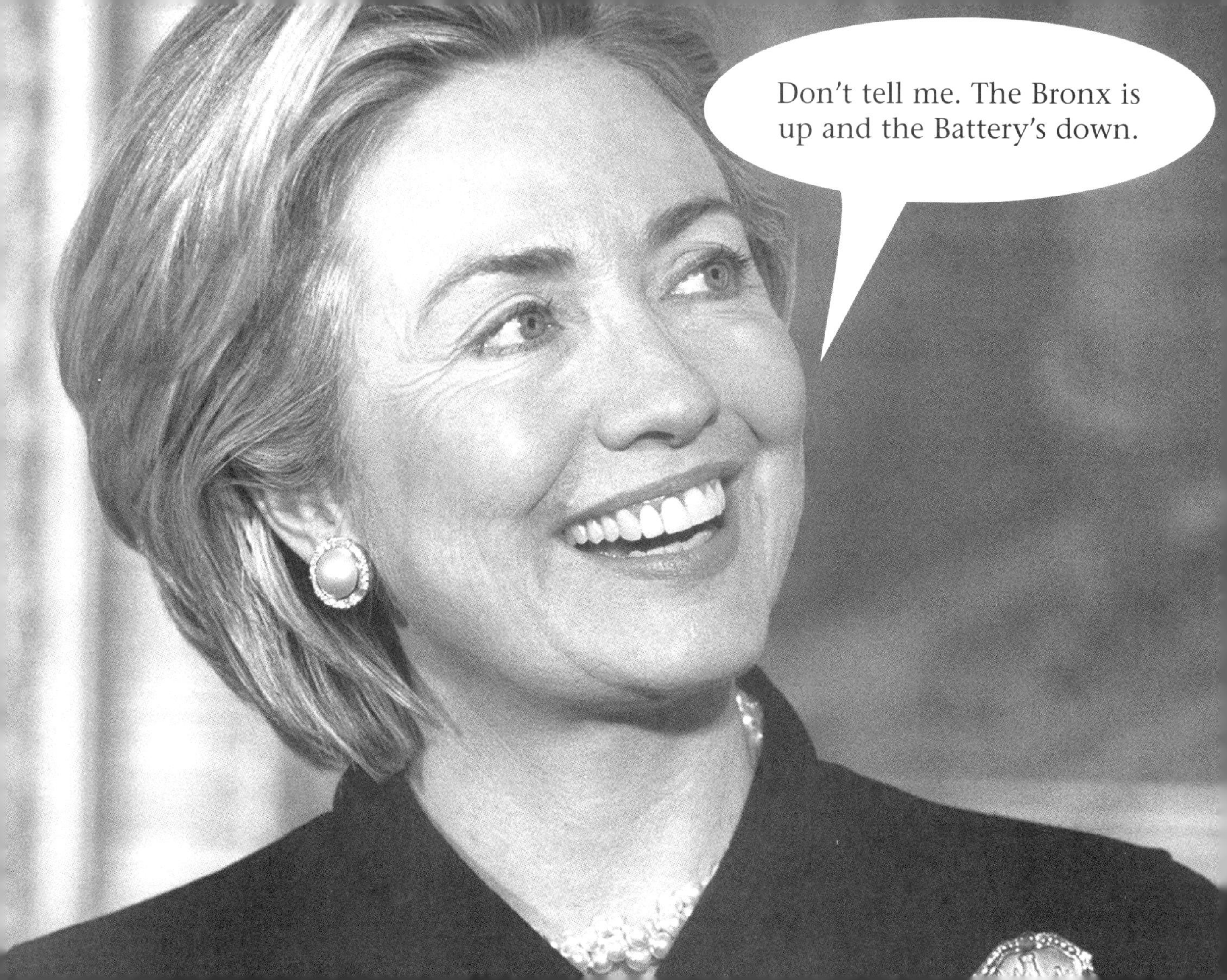
Don't tell me. The Bronx is up and the Battery's down.

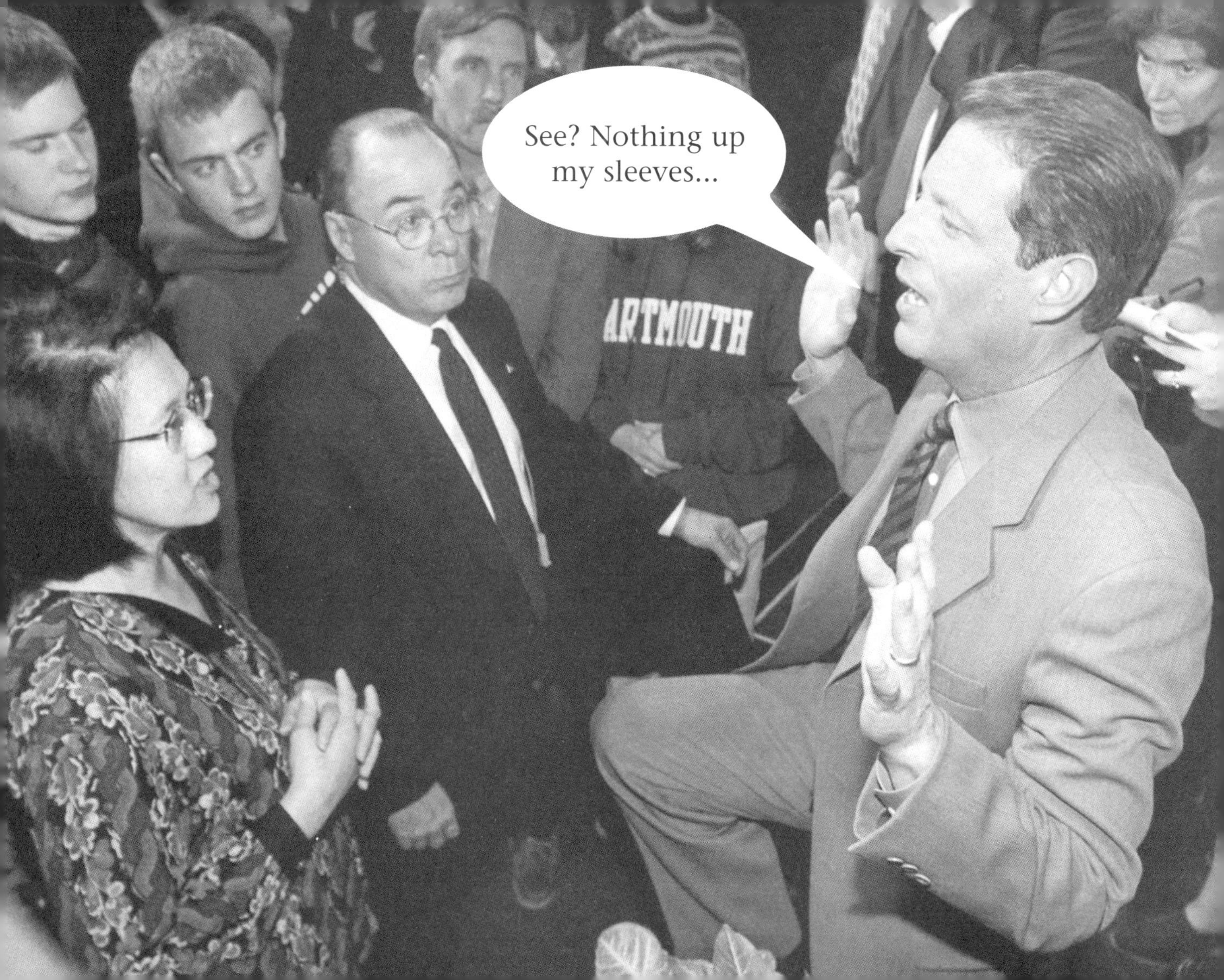
See? Nothing up my sleeves...
ARTMOUTH

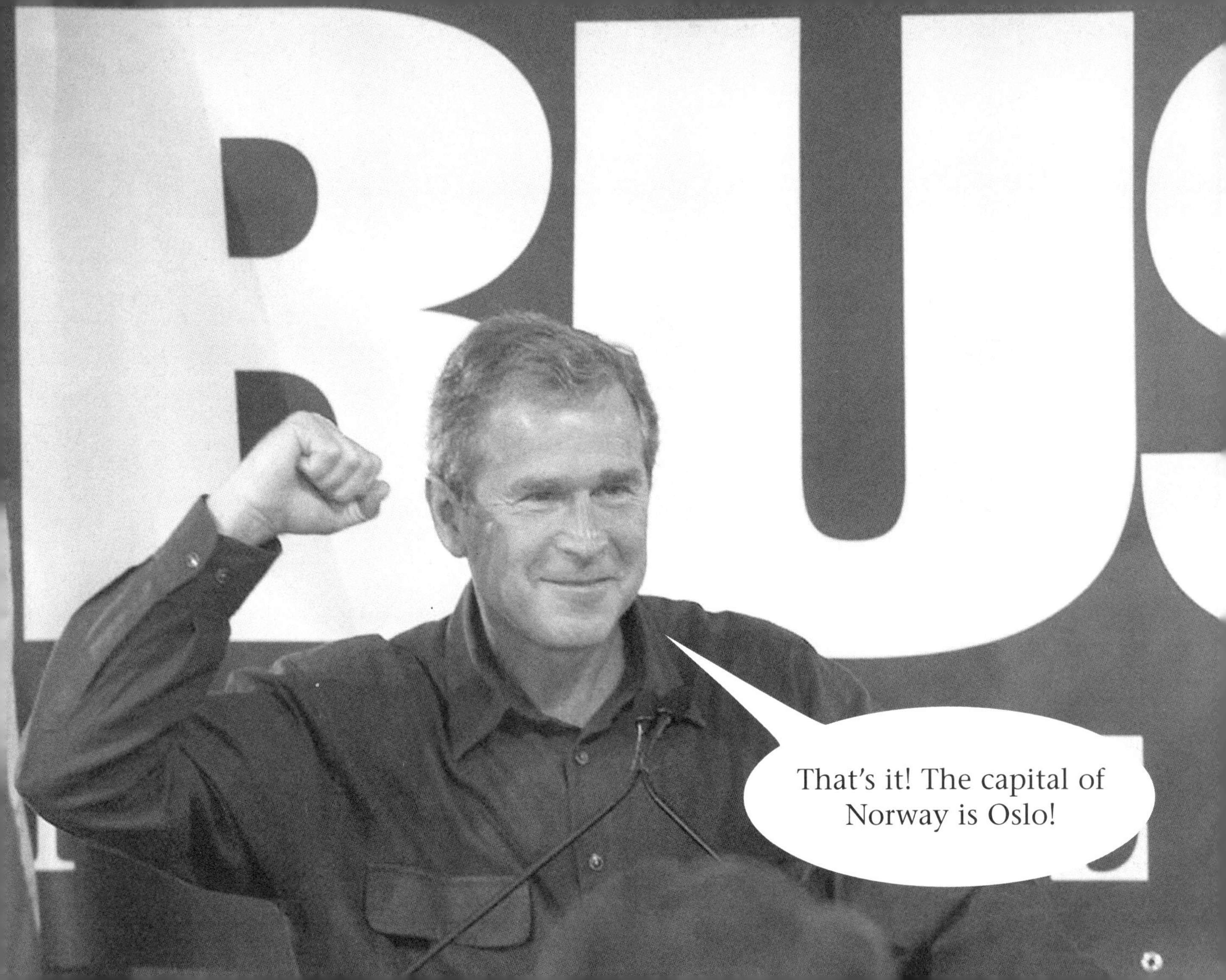
That's it! The capital of Norway is Oslo!

So the Devil said, “Pat, I will make you young again, but you must forfeit your soul.”

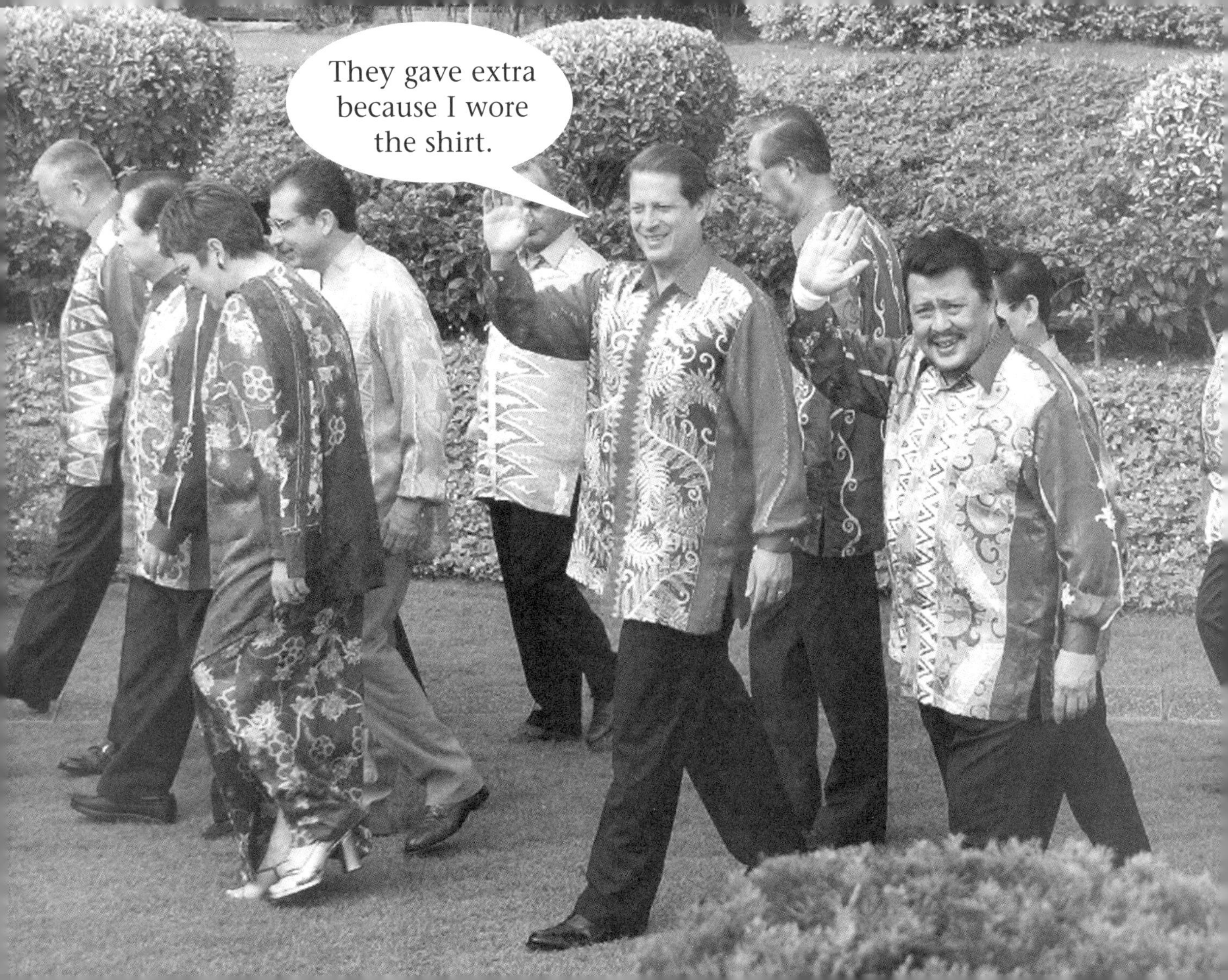
They gave extra because I wore the shirt.

If this doesn't make the papers, Orrin, I think you'd better drop out.

End Freeway
½ MILE
I suppose there may be one or two people who know more about foreign affairs than Gov. Bush.

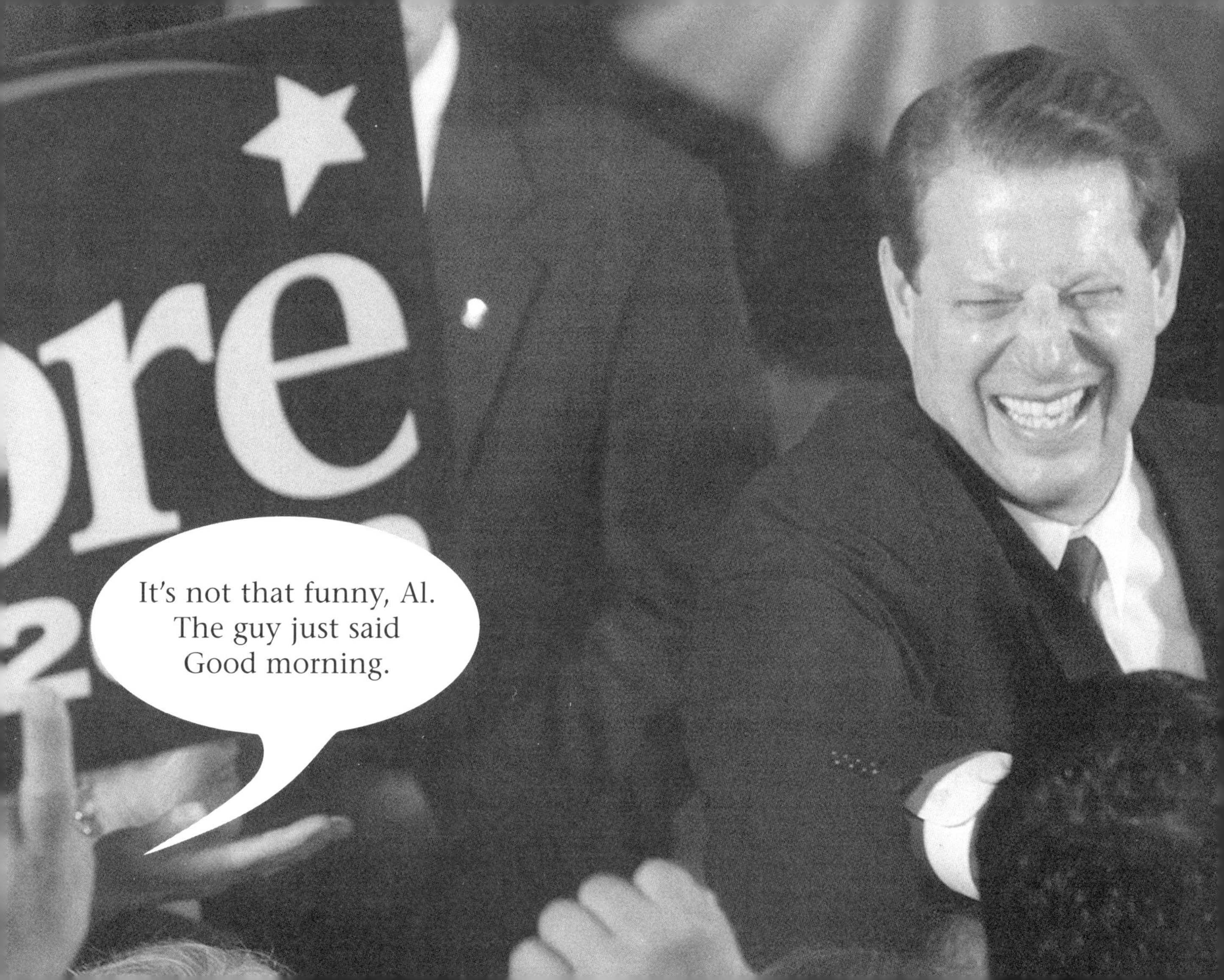
It's not that funny, Al.
The guy just said
Good morning.

Their suits are off the rack.

> They say I'm nothing without my advisers. That is absolutely, completely... Carl, what's the word I'm looking for?

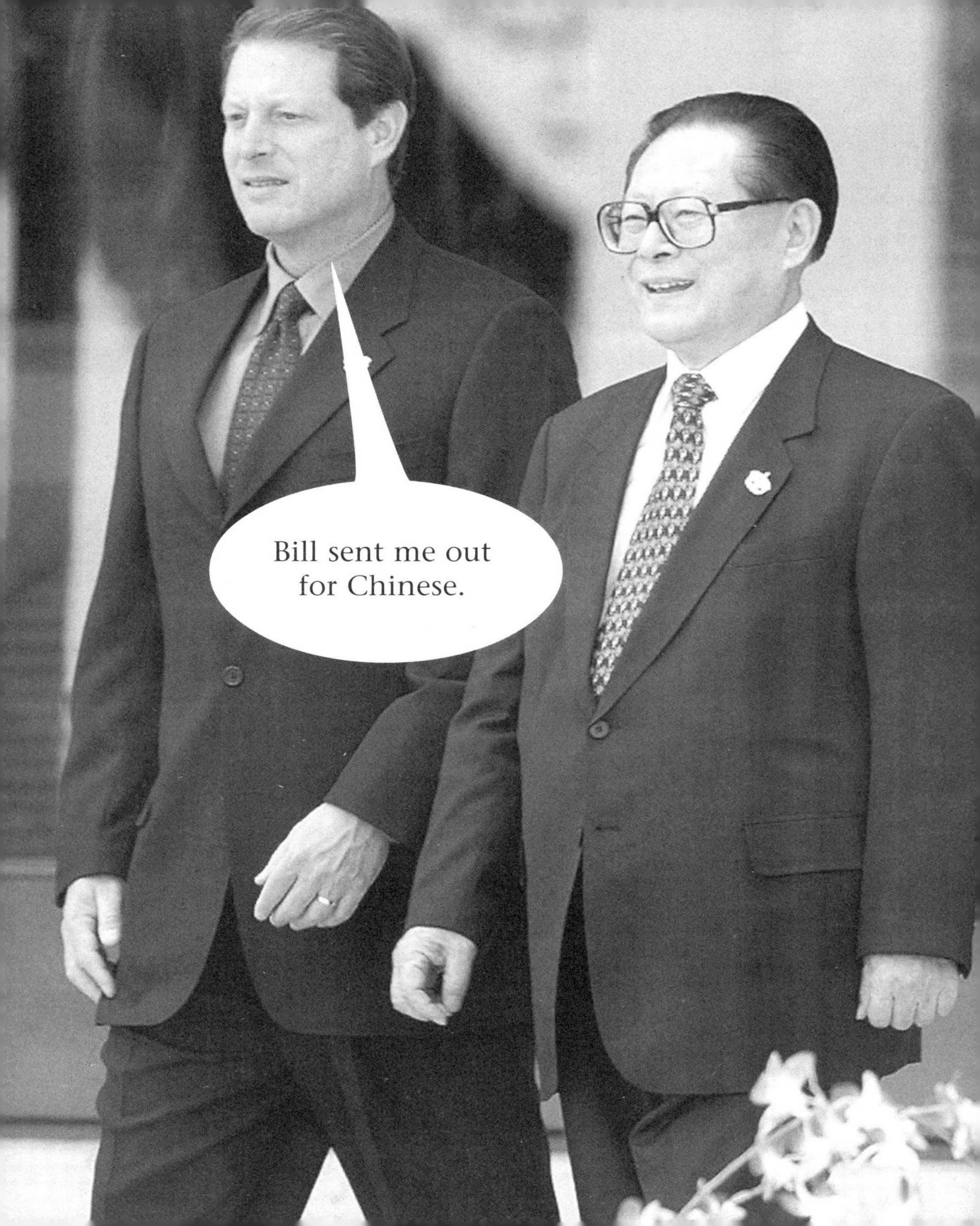
Bill sent me out
for Chinese.

Sure I'm tiresome, but I'm *decent*.

> So what? *Ike* had a temper. *Johnson* had a temper. *Attila* had a temper–

I am trying very hard not to hurt the image of professional wrestling.

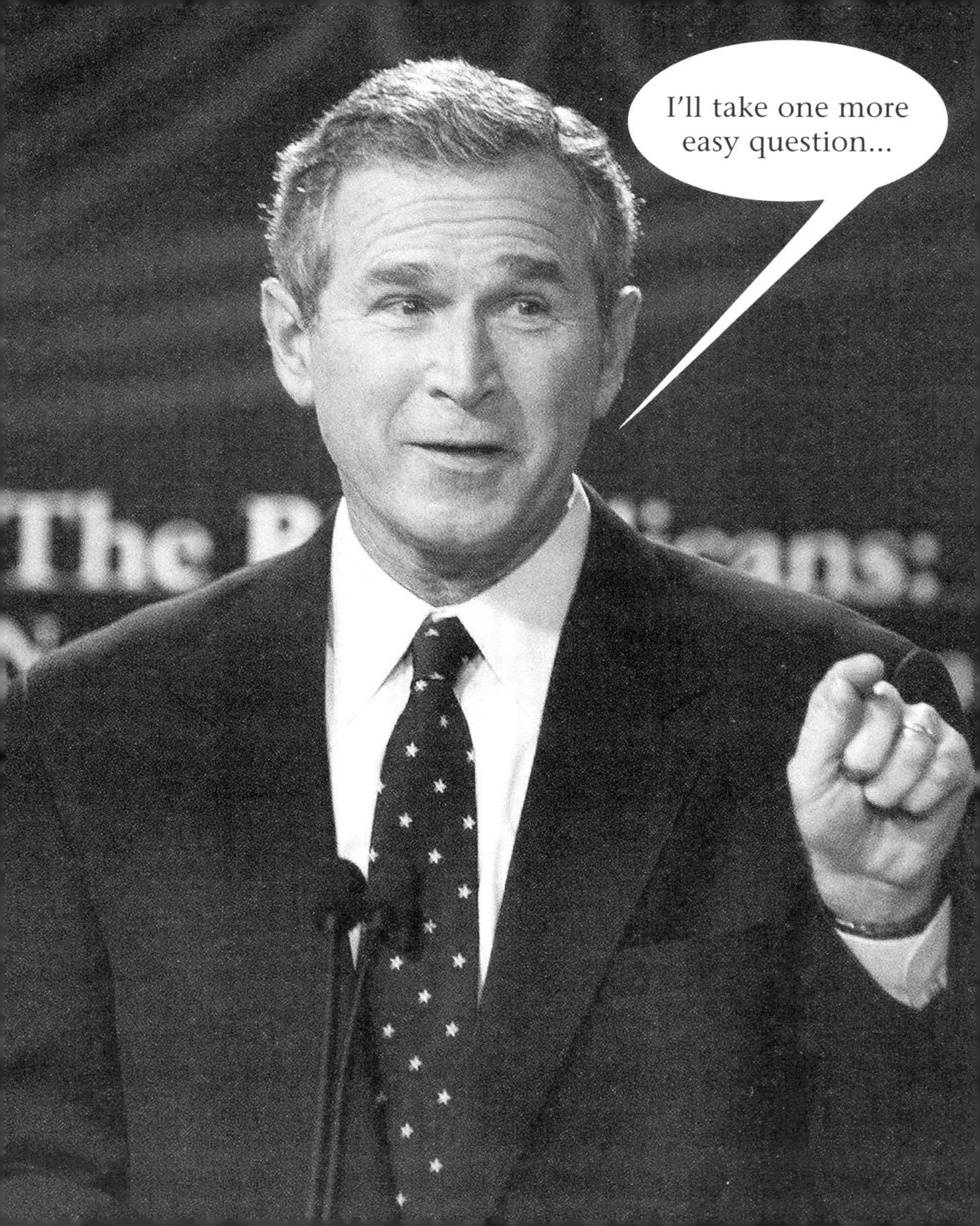
I'll take one more easy question...

"I *know* I called him one of our greatest presidents. But what I *meant* was..."

Yes, you from the New York Post with the tiny propeller on your hat.

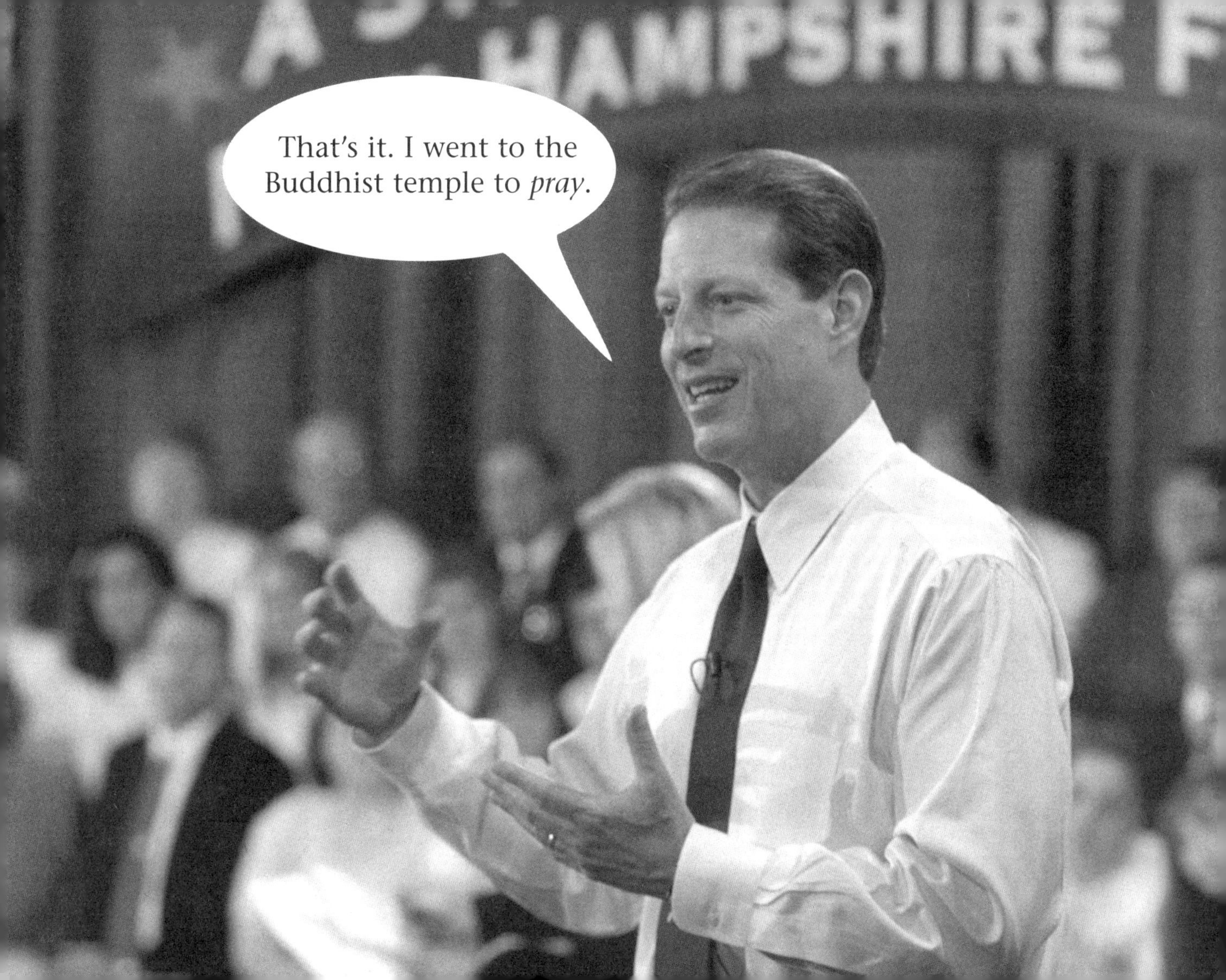
That's it. I went to the Buddhist temple to *pray*.
HAMPSHIRE

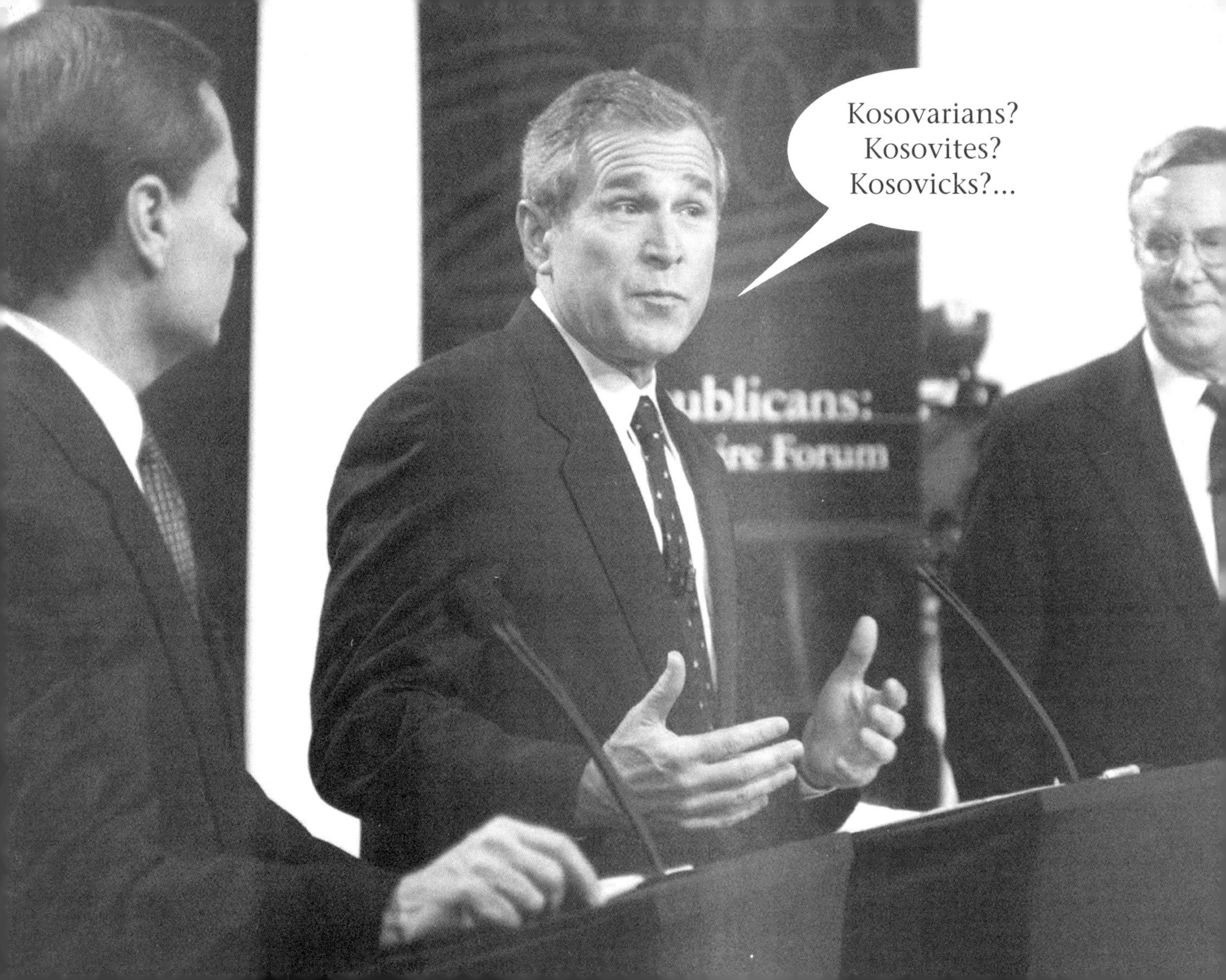
Kosovarians?
Kosovites?
Kosovicks?...

We go on the air at midnight, Governor. That's when the big hand is on the twelve...
WCCO

ARIZONA REPUBLICAN PARTY
www.azgop.org
Is that your final answer?

She'd be a good vice-president for Bush, but would she find enough for him to do?

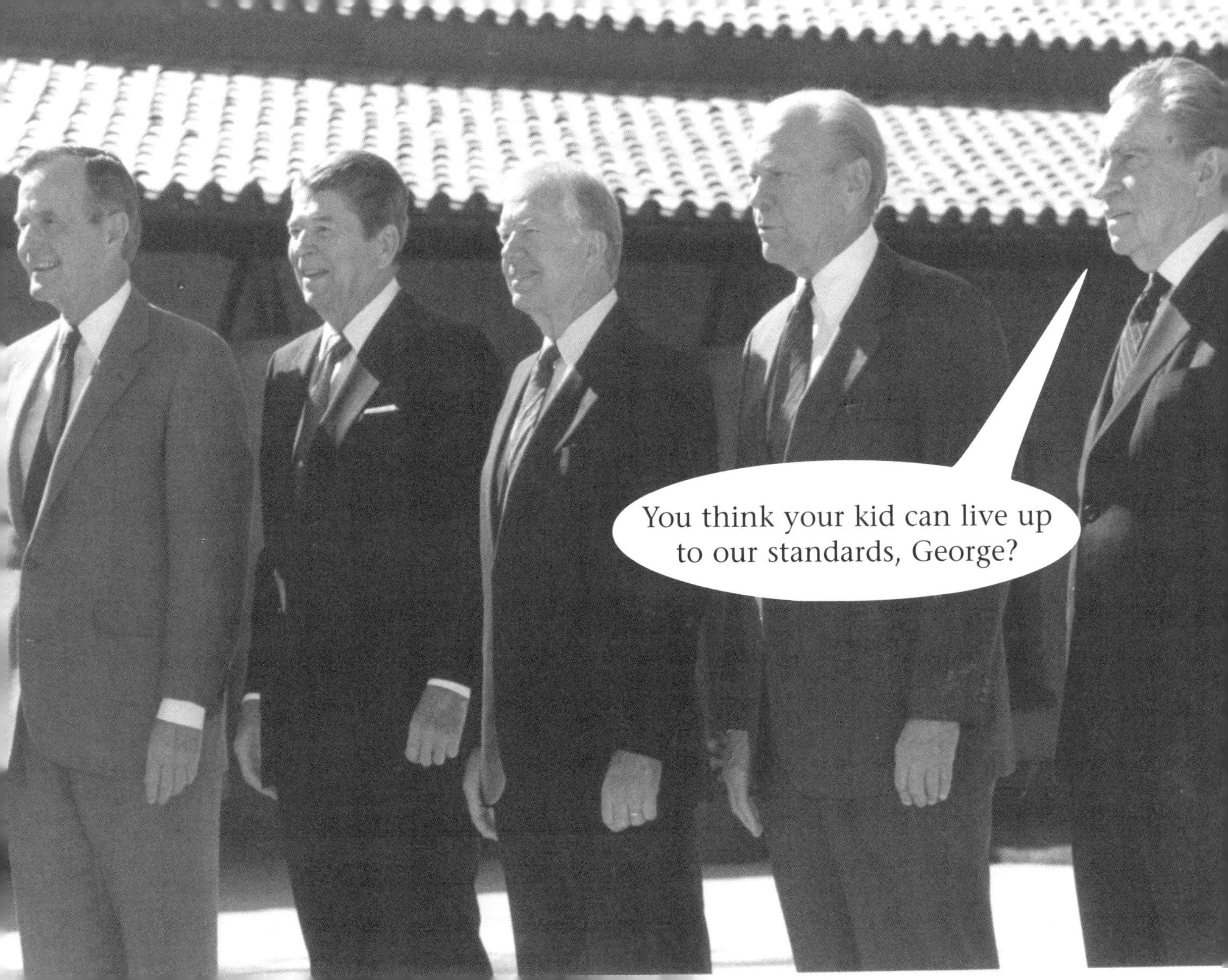
You think your kid can live up to our standards, George?

Well, if your tax plan is so reliable, why do you have to count on your fingers?

Well frankly I don't see that the flat tax works that well for us.

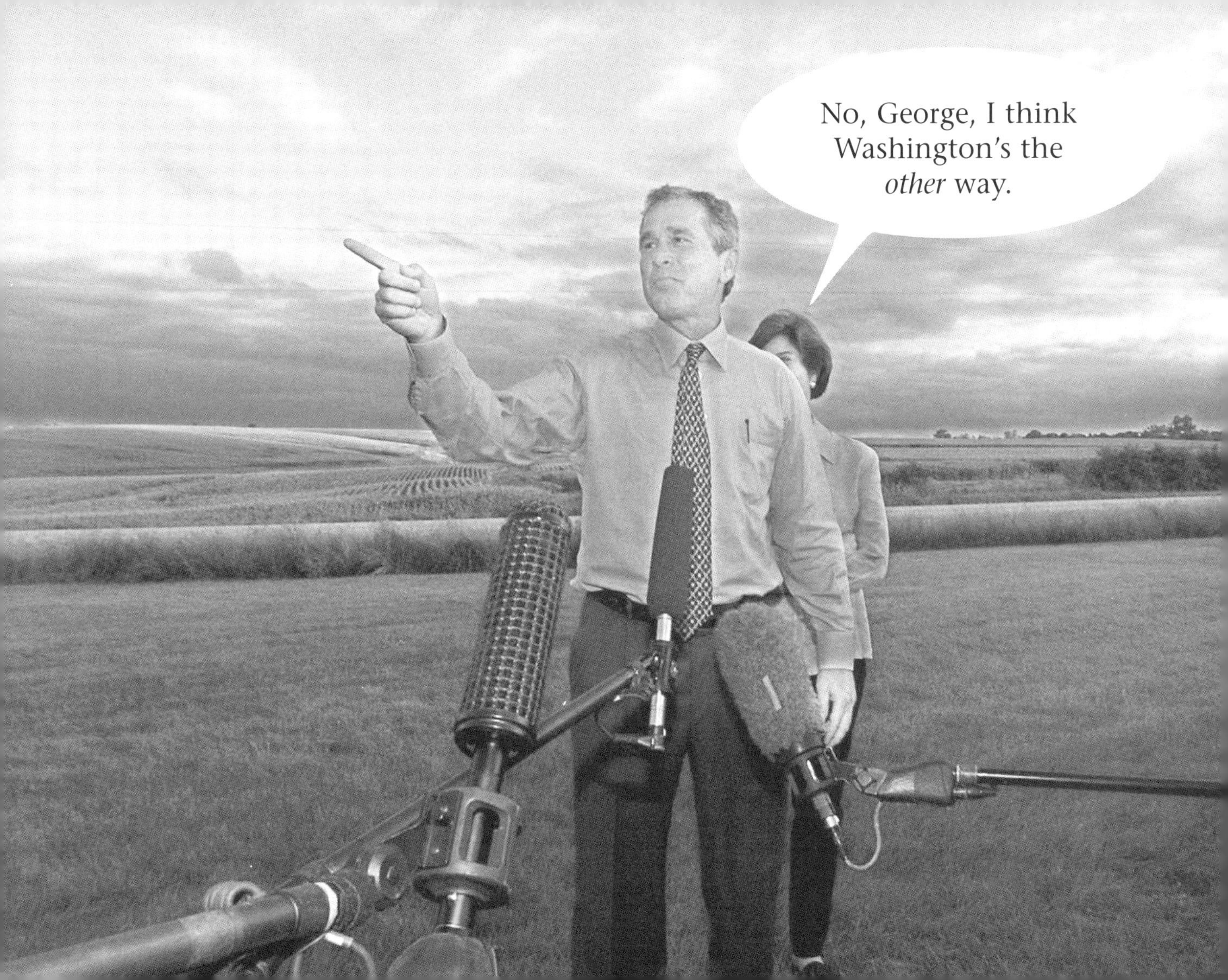
No, George, I think Washington's the *other* way.

Tallfellow Press

Los Angeles